WHY ARE THE RAIN FORESTS VANISHING?

BY ISAAC ASIMOV

Gareth Stevens Publishing
MILWAUKEE

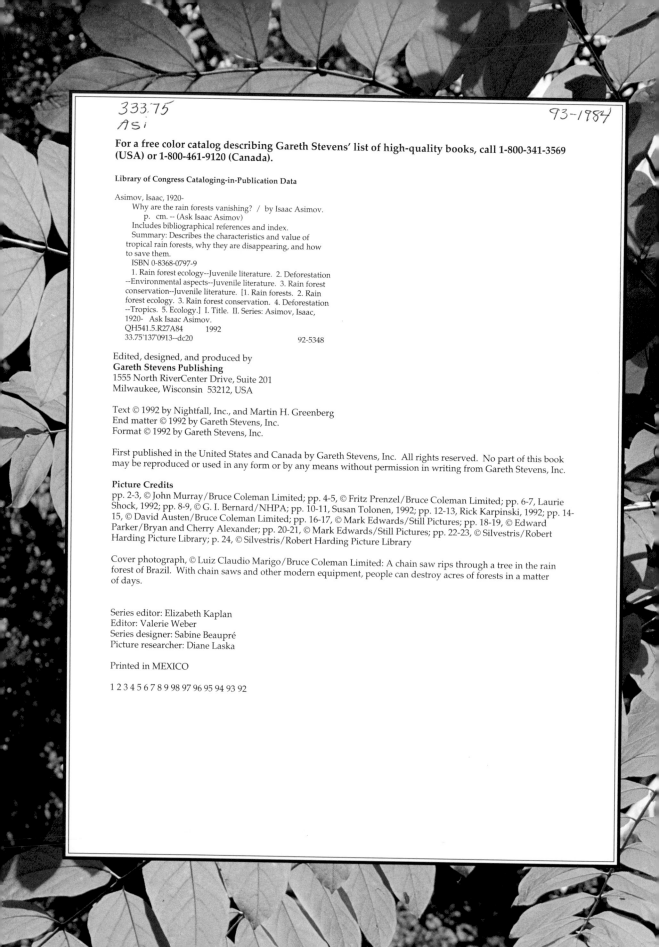

For a free color catalog describing Gareth Stevens' list of high-quality books, call 1-800-341-3569 (USA) or 1-800-461-9120 (Canada).

Library of Congress Cataloging-in-Publication Data

Asimov, Isaac, 1920-
    Why are the rain forests vanishing? / by Isaac Asimov.
      p. cm. -- (Ask Isaac Asimov)
    Includes bibliographical references and index.
    Summary: Describes the characteristics and value of
tropical rain forests, why they are disappearing, and how
to save them.
    ISBN 0-8368-0797-9
    1. Rain forest ecology--Juvenile literature. 2. Deforestation
--Environmental aspects--Juvenile literature. 3. Rain forest
conservation--Juvenile literature. [1. Rain forests. 2. Rain
forest ecology. 3. Rain forest conservation. 4. Deforestation
--Tropics. 5. Ecology.] I. Title. II. Series: Asimov, Isaac,
1920- Ask Isaac Asimov.
QH541.5.R27A84   1992
33.75'137'0913--dc20

92-5348

Edited, designed, and produced by
Gareth Stevens Publishing
1555 North RiverCenter Drive, Suite 201
Milwaukee, Wisconsin 53212, USA

Picture Credits
pp. 2-3, © John Murray/Bruce Coleman Limited; pp. 4-5, © Fritz Prenzel/Bruce Coleman Limited; pp. 6-7, Laurie Shock, 1992; pp. 8-9, © G. I. Bernard/NHPA; pp. 10-11, Susan Tolonen, 1992; pp. 12-13, Rick Karpinski, 1992; pp. 14-15, © David Austen/Bruce Coleman Limited; pp. 16-17, © Mark Edwards/Still Pictures; pp. 18-19, © Edward Parker/Bryan and Cherry Alexander; pp. 20-21, © Mark Edwards/Still Pictures; pp. 22-23, © Silvestris/Robert Harding Picture Library; p. 24, © Silvestris/Robert Harding Picture Library

Cover photograph, © Luiz Claudio Marigo/Bruce Coleman Limited: A chain saw rips through a tree in the rain forest of Brazil. With chain saws and other modern equipment, people can destroy acres of forests in a matter of days.

Series editor: Elizabeth Kaplan
Editor: Valerie Weber
Series designer: Sabine Beaupré
Picture researcher: Diane Laska

Printed in MEXICO

1 2 3 4 5 6 7 8 9 98 97 96 95 94 93 92

Contents

Words printed in **boldface** type the first time they occur in the text appear in the glossary.

Exploring Our Environment

Look around you. You see forests, fields, rivers, and oceans. You see plants, animals, trees, and birds. All of these things make up our **environment**. Sometimes there are problems with the environment. For example, people are chopping down vast areas of tropical rain forests. These forests had been standing for millions of years. What are tropical rain forests? Why are they valuable? Why are people destroying them, and why does this cause trouble? Let's find out.

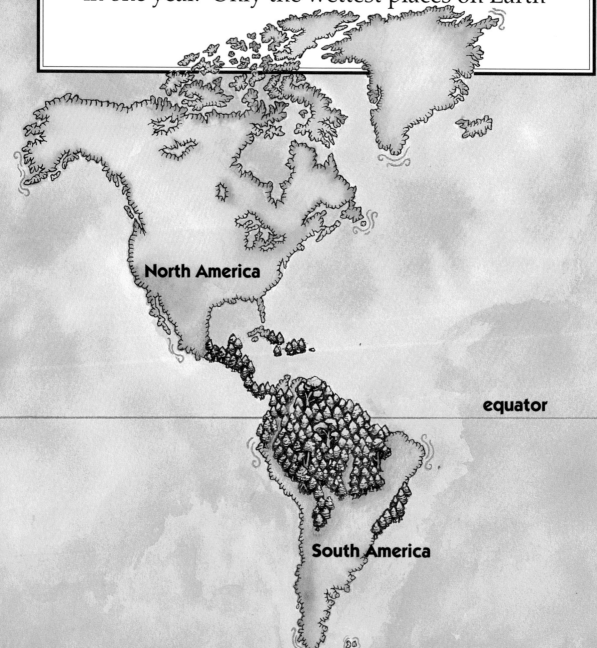

The Green Belt

Rain forests get their name because of the large amounts of rain that falls on them. As much as 200 inches (500 cm) of rain can fall in one year. Only the wettest places on Earth

North America

South America

equator

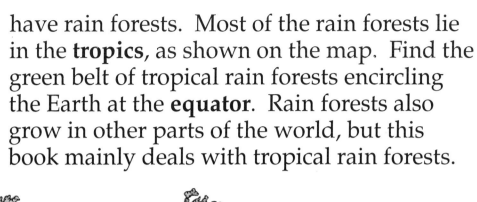

have rain forests. Most of the rain forests lie in the **tropics**, as shown on the map. Find the green belt of tropical rain forests encircling the Earth at the **equator**. Rain forests also grow in other parts of the world, but this book mainly deals with tropical rain forests.

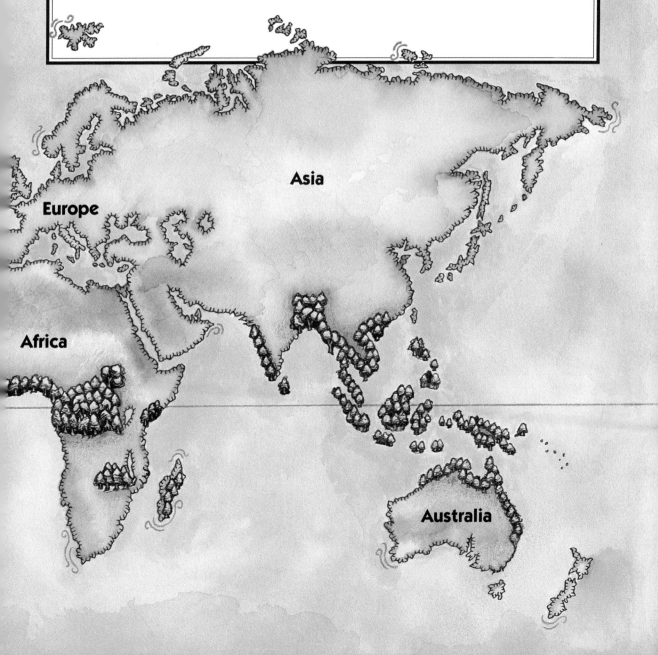

Europe

Asia

Africa

Australia

Under the Canopy

The heavy, steady rain that falls over the tropical rain forest supports lush plant life. Huge trees 100 feet (30 m) tall form a leafy **canopy.** Vines twine up the trees to get more sunlight. Plants with showy flowers grow in the forks of tree branches. A few plants that grow well in shade are sprinkled across the forest floor. But thick ground covering grows only where a lot of light comes through, for example, along riverbanks or where a fallen tree has made a hole in the canopy.

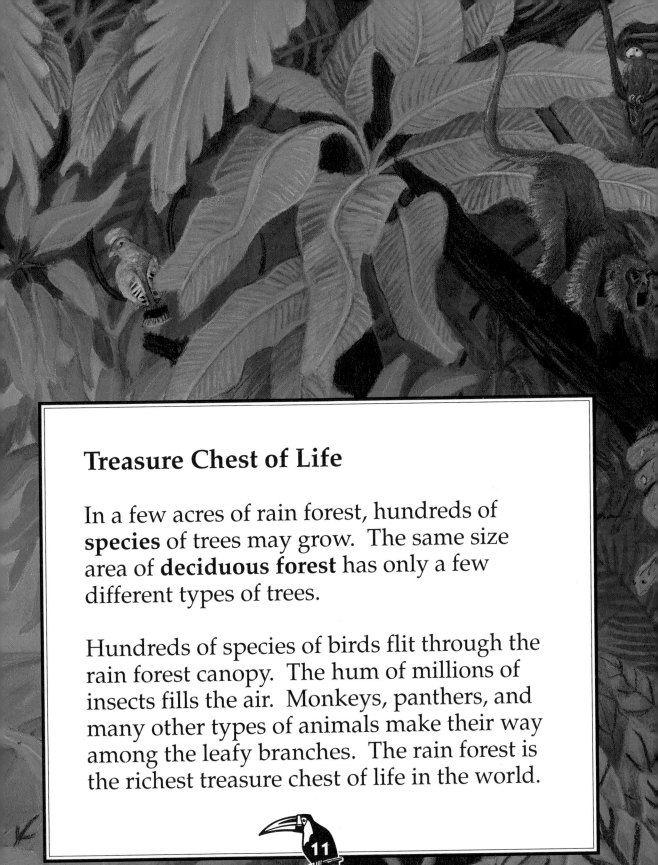

Treasure Chest of Life

In a few acres of rain forest, hundreds of **species** of trees may grow. The same size area of **deciduous forest** has only a few different types of trees.

Hundreds of species of birds flit through the rain forest canopy. The hum of millions of insects fills the air. Monkeys, panthers, and many other types of animals make their way among the leafy branches. The rain forest is the richest treasure chest of life in the world.

Enriching and Balancing the Earth

People also find treasures of plant life in the rain forest. Bananas, cinnamon, coffee, rice — all grow from rain forest plants. These plants also give us medicines to fight many diseases.

Even more importantly, plants take in **carbon dioxide** and give off **oxygen**. Because plant growth is so lush there, rain forests are very important in balancing these gases in the **atmosphere**. Without this balance, our climate would warm up. Plants and animals throughout the world would suffer.

Going Up in Smoke

Sadly, these valuable rain forests could vanish in your lifetime. In the past 30 years, more than half of the world's rain forests have been destroyed. And each year even more of these lush lands disappear. People burn the forests to make farmland. They cut down the trees for lumber. They bulldoze large areas to build cattle ranches. Oil drillers in the rain forest dump **toxic wastes** on the ground and in streams. These wastes kill off plants and animals in the rain forest.

14

Never to Grow Back

People lived in the rain forests for thousands of years without destroying them. They cleared small plots of land and planted their crops. After a few years, when the soil was no longer fertile, they abandoned their fields and the rain forest quickly grew back.

But today, people are clearing such large areas of the rain forest the forest can't grow back. Heavy rains quickly wash away the thin layers of soil, and the land becomes barren. The once teeming rain forest turns into a wasteland.

Who's at Fault?

Many people who live near the rain forests are clearing the land to make money farming, ranching, and logging. Many of the crops grown here and the beef from the ranches are shipped mainly to the United States, Canada, and Europe. The lumber is made into furniture and paper and shipped north as well.

So, we are all to blame for the destruction of the rain forest. Even if we are not the ones cutting down the trees, we use the things that come from clearing this valuable land.

18

How Can We Save the Rain Forests?

Most importantly, we can save them by not using products that come from cleared rain forest land. Many of the items your family buys may be made of wood that comes from rain forest trees. Ask them not to buy these products. Use less paper and recycle what you do use. Eat less **imported** beef.

Another important thing to do is to support organizations that are trying to stop rain forest destruction. Join conservation groups that are working to **preserve** the rain forests.

21

The Clock Is Ticking

With every second that goes by, an area of rain forest the size of a football field is destroyed! With this destruction, thousands of plant and animal species vanish. Any one of these may hold an unfound cure for cancer or other deadly diseases. We can't afford to lose the rain forests. They bring great beauty and richness to the Earth and help preserve the balance of life on our precious planet.

22

More Books to Read

Explore a Tropical Forest by Donald J. Crump (National Geographic)
Rain Forest by Helen Coucher (Farrar, Straus & Giroux)
Vanishing Rain Forests by Paula Hogan (Gareth Stevens)

Places to Write

Here are some places you can write to for more information about
tropical rain forests.   Be sure to tell them exactly what you want to
know about.   Give them your full name and address so that they
can write back to you.

Rainforest Alliance
270 Lafayette Street
New York, NY 10012

Greenpeace
2623 West 4th Avenue
Vancouver, BC V6K 1P8

Glossary

atmosphere (AT-muh-sfear): the gases that surround the Earth.

canopy (CAN-uh-pee): the topmost layer of plant life in the rain
forest; the canopy forms a thick layer of leaves and branches
high above the ground.

carbon dioxide: a gas in the Earth's atmosphere that contains one
atom of carbon and two atoms of oxygen; carbon dioxide traps
heat close to the Earth.

deciduous forest (dih-SIJ-uh-wus): forests of trees that shed their
leaves in winter; deciduous forests are common in temperate
parts of the world, such as North America's Pacific Northwest.

environment (en-VIE-run-ment): the natural and humanmade
things that make up the Earth.

23

equator (ee-KWAY-ter): an imaginary line that runs around the Earth halfway between the North and South Poles.

imported (ihm-PORT-uhd): referring to a product shipped in from another country.

oxygen (AHK-sih-jen): a colorless, odorless gas that makes up about one-fifth of the Earth's atmosphere; we need oxygen to live.

preserve (pruh-ZERV): to save or keep in its present form.

species (SPEE-sheez): a group of animals or plants that are all considered to be of the same type; tropical rain forests have more species of plants and animals than any other environment on our planet.

toxic waste: any waste that can cause serious disease and that poisons the environment.

tropics (TRAH-picks): the warmest region of the Earth; it lies near the equator.

Index

24